NIFTY
NEIGHBORS

Mister Rogers
and
Jesus Christ

TRACY EMERICK, Ph.D.

Primix Publishing
East Brunswick Office Evolution
1 Tower Center Boulevard, Ste 1510
East Brunswick, NJ 08816
www.primixpublishing.com
Phone: 1-800-538-5788

Published by Primix Publishing: 11/12/2025

ISBN: 979-8-89194-584-5(sc)
ISBN: 979-8-89194-585-2(e)

Any people depicted in stock imagery provided by iStock are models, and such images are being used for illustrative purposes only.

Certain stock imagery © iStock.

Contents

Dedication:
To my brother-in-law, Mike Buchner

INTRODUCTION

Love your neighbor as yourself.

This basic quote from the Bible is imprinted in our minds and hearts for a very long time. Sounds simple but is difficult to execute. Let's admit it. As years go by, the population has become more different than alike. We are opposing poles but never attract. The brightest and richest people in this world created technology and new advancements to connect us together but we become – even more – disconnected. The world created an organized structure for humanity, but it caused humanity to gain ideologies and ideas that divide rather than unite. We have an endless list of differences: personality, character, background, race, color, political opinions, religious beliefs, and ideologies. The list becomes longer each day which brings me to a conclusion: there are more reasons to believe that *loving our neighbor as yourself* is now becoming close to impossible.

The more we move forward to the future, the more this basic guideline becomes complex and complicated. We often debate about the smallest differences, we complicate the little stuff, and oftentimes, we need validation of the correctness of our stance. We want to be proven right. We thirst for validation. With these in mind, I am inclined to believe that *loving thy neighbor* is like a mathematical equation most people cannot solve. And that equation becomes harder to solve every day.

The bright side, however, is the fact that there were personalities who walked the face of this earth whose teachings rekindle our faith in the harmony of humanity. When we look at each of their lives, we realize that the seeming equation that divides us needs no complex solution. These personalities touched so many lives and inspired many souls by straightening the tangled pieces, giving us the simplest form of solution to *loving thy neighbor*. These personalities left the earth with a legacy that served as a model for how we should live our lives at present.

This book will uncover the life and works of two personalities that brought new perspectives worth studying and living - *Mr. Fred*

Rogers and Jesus Christ.

Mr. Fred Rogers, commonly known as Mister Rogers in the American TV Show *"Mister Rogers' Neighborhood,"* is a TV host, author, and pastor. For more than 30 years, Mister Rogers cemented a relationship with millions of children across the globe with his uniquely different concept of engaging children as he portrays himself as a good and trusted neighbor. Mister Rogers looked directly into the camera as he speaks to his audience and sang beautiful songs with lessons that hit the core of children's hearts. His radical kindness, acceptance, and empathy created a place that as TV Guide described: *"… makes us, young and old alike, feel safe, cared for and valued… Wherever Mister Rogers is, so is sanctuary."*

Jesus Christ, on the other hand, changed the concept of love by introducing a form of *radical love* – loving the sinners, the unrighteous, and the unholy by spreading the message of *loving thy neighbor* (regardless of who you are) as a guiding path to harmony and salvation from sins. Jesus, called the "Messiah" or the Messenger was born more than 2000 years ago, and created ideology-altering miracles and life-changing parables that steered the direction away from the traditions of the old times towards a more accepting form of love that eventually cost His own human life.

Both personalities provided us with the best concepts of good neighbors anchored on love, care, and compassion which brought influence on the lives of billions, and created a perfect, new direction for the current generation to follow.

But with the current state of our generation – a generation filled with selflessness and diversity in opinion and ideologies, where every person strives for recognition, power, and validation for correctness, how can we be guided back to the path that leads to a better synthesis of ideas and beliefs? How can we become good neighbors to those who oppose our beliefs? How can we become friends with those that often disagree with our opinions? How do we become a good neighbor?

This is what this book is all about. It is my hope that when you flip the last page of this book, you become a better neighbor yourself and you are encouraged to share this piece of material with your neighbors, too.

CHAPTER ONE
What's a Neighbor?

Being a good neighbor is an art that makes life richer.
– Gladys Taber

Growing up, we are likely to hear the word neighbor in everyday conversations. This time, let's go deep into the etymology and meaning of the word. The word "neighbor" can be divided into two different Old English words *"neah"* and *"gabur."* The word *"neah"* means *near* and the word *"gabur"* means *dweller.* Together this creates the word neighbor or someone who dwells near.

If you list down your neighbors, you'd probably have a long list of them. But what if I tell you to list down only your "good neighbors," your list surely shortens.

Nifty neighbors are people whom you shared fond memories with and who showed you the best qualities of a neighbor. These people created a great perception in your mind – it could be a childhood friend, a next-door neighbor who shared their food with you, that friendly classmate who defended you from bullies or helped you with your school projects, or that kind and generous teacher who encouraged you to do better. Our minds have imprinted an image of a good neighbor through them. Through these people, we have a personified image of a good neighbor. Forever, they take up a huge space that continually inspires us because of their selflessness and acts of kindness.

Neighbor, Defined

The word neighbor is defined in many ways with one common thought. Linguistically speaking, it is defined in three parts of speech: as a noun, an adjective, and as a verb.

As defined by Merriam-Webster, the word neighbor as a noun means *"one located near another."* As an adjective, it means, *"being immediately adjoining or relatively near."* As a verb, it means *"to adjoin immediately or lie relatively near to"*. But the word neighbor as an intransitive verb means to *"associate in a neighborly way"* with the term "neighborly" meaning being connected with a feeling of friendliness and congeniality.

Looking at these terms and definitions, there involves an element of distance. A neighbor is someone who is in close proximity to someone. But once the word is used as an intransitive verb – an action word – the strong and personal "additional element" is involved – that is *friendship*.

The Marks of a Good Neighbor

A true, good, and nifty neighbor, therefore, is not only someone close to you in terms of distance, but someone who extends to you his friendship and creates camaraderie. A nifty neighbor is someone who looks after, cares for, and helps you without asking for any return. He looks after your betterment and for your safety. With this, a relationship is created, and the good neighbor constantly strives to grow it.

Let me share two inspiring, timeless stories that really made a mark recently about nifty neighbors. This way, we will put a spotlight on the actions done by these nifty neighbors that set them apart from others:

The Story of Quinn Waters

Readers Digest posted this inspiring story of a nifty neighbor who changed someone's life: Quinn Waters has seen a lot of tough things in his short three years of life. So when the preschooler was put in isolation in his home as part of his treatment for brain cancer, his family prepared themselves to help him endure one more heartbreaking hardship. But then the Waters' neighbors stepped in, deciding that while they couldn't do anything about the cancer, they could certainly keep Quinn entertained. At first, it was just nearby friends doing silly puppet shows, juggling, singing, and playing games outside the large window where the little boy watched, delighted.

As word spread, however, more and more people showed up— from the community and then from around the country. Quinn, nicknamed "The Mighty Quinn," and his family have now been visited by athletes, police departments, dance teams, and he even got his own private concert from the Dropkick Murphys, all from his "quindow." "The fact that there's so much bad news, you see something like this and everybody wants to get on board with it. No one wants to see a little kid be sick," his father Jarlath Waters told the TV network, Fox. "Every single person who has shown up has done wonders for him."

Nifty neighbors, therefore, change lives. They will go above and beyond the usual neighborly act to turn your sad situations into happy ones. They are your brothers and sisters who are unrelated to you by affinity but show the same brotherly and sisterly care.

Life doesn't always give us the good stuff. We will be faced with so many harsh realities and situations, but a nifty neighbor will stick with you to make those situations lighter. They will make you feel better about yourself, whatever the situation you face.

Isn't it amazing to have a nifty neighbor?

The Nifty Grocery Neighbor

There is a recent trend in social media about people paying for groceries for their neighbors. One anonymous viral story reads, "I was in line at Aldi and this girl with two toddlers in front of me had her card declined and she looked so sad and said 'let me call my husband real quick' and it was only $18, so I just paid for it, and she was very sweet and then as she walked off, the lady behind me said 'You know that was probably a scam, right' and like, even if it was, like what a sad scam, right? $18 at the Aldi. If you're 'scamming' me for some Tyson chicken and apple juice and cauliflower, then just take my money."

Actress Ashley Westover was so moved by this story and dozens like it that she posted a compilation to her Facebook with the reminder to "Do good recklessly!" As shown in the hundreds of comments, the stories have since motivated many others to pay for their neighbor's groceries.

In this story, we learn that a good and nifty neighbor revives our faith in humanity. When someone is in need, others could just simply turn a blind eye, but a nifty neighbor's heart will always find a way to ease others' situations. A nifty neighbor's heart is always in the right place.

Disneyworld or Food for Evacuees?

Natural disasters have a way of making people depend on their neighbors in a way nothing else does and the results can be incredibly moving—as six-year-old Jermaine Bell proves. The boy had been saving money with his family for a dream trip to Disneyworld when their neighborhood was suddenly ordered to evacuate before Hurricane Dorian hit the South Carolina town.

Immediately the first-grader decided that he'd rather use his hard-earned cash to help his neighbors flee the storm than for a vacation. Jermaine stood alongside a nearby road handing out hundreds of chips, hot dogs, and bottles of water to evacuees. He even stopped to pray with neighbors who were scared or worried. "I wanted them to have some food to eat, so they can enjoy the ride to the place that they're going to stay at," he told the News Channel WJBF. "I wanted to be generous and live to give."

Reading these nifty neighbor stories brings hope that despite the bad things happening around us, we see a glimmer of light that it is possible to uplift one another. Amidst all of these, good neighbor stories continually spark the light in our lives.

So, let's share it. Live it. It is contagious.

The Quest to Become a Nifty Neighbor

So, let me challenge you: Have we shown the same good *neighborly* act to someone today? Have we been good and nifty neighbors?

Well, this book is written for everyone – young and old – because you and I are "nifty neighbors *in progress*." And the more we listen to stories of good and nifty neighbors, we revive our hope in humanity. When we hear these nifty neighbor true stories, we realize that it is possible to personify the qualities of a good neighbor. But I firmly believe that to achieve that, we must look at the highest standard of nifty neighbors that we can only find in Mister Rogers and Jesus Christ.

The more we study those two personalities in this book, the more we draw ourselves to their good nature and hopefully personify their good works, as our initial step to developing the *neighborly* persona.

As we go through the pages of this book, it is my hope that we personify the nifty neighbors whose lives we will expose in this book.

CHAPTER TWO
Won't You Be My Neighbor?

"It's a day in this neighborhood, A beautiful day for a neighbor,
Would you be mine?
Could you be mine?"

Mr. Fred Rogers or Mister Rogers in the famous American TV program, *"Mister Rogers' Neighborhood,"* one of the longest- running TV programs in television history, starts his show with an invitational song. This song marks the opening of the program:

"It's a day in this neighborhood,
A beautiful day for a neighbor,
Would you be mine?
Could you be mine?
It's a neighborly day in this beautywood,
A neighborly day for a beauty,
Would you be mine?
Could you be mine?
I have always wanted to have a neighbor just like you,
I've always wanted to live in a neighborhood with you."
I have always wanted to have a neighbor just like you
I've always wanted to live in a neighborhood with you
Let's make the most of this beautiful day
Since we're together, might as well say
Would you be my, could you be my...
Won't you be my neighbor?

These are lines of the opening song of Mister Rogers' Neighborhood which became an anthem to many children across the world from the 1960s until the 1990s – an anthem of invitation to the show that brings thrill to children and memories to millions. Played in 870 episodes for three long decades, the song captured the attention of children, inviting them to become Mister Rogers' neighbor.

I am always impressed with the brilliant way Mister Rogers entices viewers, young and old, by capturing them through a song to invite them with each "visit". Those who have watched his episodes know this routine so well: he enters through a door with his *coat and tie* as Mister Rogers sings the first few lines of the song. He moves to his closet and dons his *sweater*. He moves towards the couch and changes his leather shoes to *sneakers*. He finishes the song and starts his story.

That *donning of the sweater and sneakers* is known to be the signal of transformation from Fred Rogers to Mister Rogers. But for me, there is an even deeper meaning to this which we can all learn from. First, the "costume change" sets the environment to a more comfortable and calm place by changing his attire which gave a sense of a welcoming, inviting, and humble environment. Second, it surely contributed to entertainment and it sparked curiosity. It is believed that when someone tells a story and there is some sort of action behind it, it doubles the attention attraction.

But more than just the setting of a comfortable environment or capturing viewers' attention, there is a third and most important element to this action. The *donning of the sweater and sneakers* gives a strong symbolism that is tied to Mister Rogers' power of persuasion.

Figure 1: A stamp shows portrait of Fred McFeely Rogers (1928- 2003), series Forever, 2018.

Leaving Our Old Self and the Power of Persuasion

I would love to start this book the same way Mister Rogers started his show. I believe the third important symbolism or message that the *donning of sweater and sneakers* have is this: regardless of your personal success, wealth, or economic status, being welcoming, inviting, humble, and kind are the necessary foundations of becoming a good neighbor.

There is a fourth meaning to this symbolism, however, which is tied to the third: Mister Rogers blended two elements: a sense of *command and authority* and the *sense of humility and friendship*, altogether. Analyzing how he begins his storytelling, we see the great and noble extremes in Mister Rogers' personality combined. He comes out of the door with his coat and tie which symbolizes trustworthiness and professionalism (command and authority), and he then changes his clothing to a *sweater and sneakers* which symbolizes this warm and layback personality (humility and friendship). But again, the third symbolism is the most powerful of all. The third symbolism brings a powerful message to his viewers that I believe elevated him to decades of worldwide fame: *Regardless of who I am, I am a friend, I am your neighbor, I want you to be with me.*

Figure 2: Mr. Rogers dons his sweater marking the start of the program, Mister Rogers' Neighborhood.

Here, we realize how impactful it is to be one with your audiences simply by providing visual signals. While it is important to be listened to, it is important to note *the way* we take our listeners to listen. When we strive to become nifty neighbors, we ought to *don our own* sweaters *and sneakers*. We leave our status behind and become equals with others.

Jesus Dons His Sweater and Sneakers, Too

This entrance can be likened to our other nifty neighbor, Jesus Christ. Jesus, like Mister Rogers, starts His story through what Christians believe as the Divine transformed to human life. Studying the Christian icon, Jesus, he made entrance to the world similarly – He holds the highest authority but dons a human body to amplify a message to the world: *Regardless of who I am, I am a friend, I am a neighbor, and I want you to be with Me.*

It is important to note that Jesus' entrance to the world (based on the world's standards) was truly unimpressive. But that same unimpressive entrance brought Him to become the world's most popular religious icon. We cannot deny that Jesus' unimpressive entrance in the *poorest form* was the very reason why Christianity is undoubtedly the biggest religion. Jesus was born out of a manger, a place where animals live, to show the world that He is one with the poor, the less privileged, the lowly, and the helpless. He was a son of a carpenter. He was born in the small town of Nazareth. He was raised in a poor town with less access to water and agriculture, without any thriving industry. It was literally an unknown territory to the world.

You see, Jesus donned his own *sweater and sneakers* like Mister Rogers at the very beginning of His story – an astounding display of humility, empathy, friendship, and warmth. Regardless of who He is, he became equal with the people. This, alone, sends a strong message to the world and to us, in our quest to become nifty neighbors ourselves.

Sweater and Sneakers: Donning Our Raw Selves

Mister Rogers and Jesus Christ also want us to don our own *"life sweaters and sneakers"* as we strive to become nifty neighbors. This is only possible when we leave our old selves behind and wear our raw selves. Regardless of age, color, status, beliefs, financial and social capacity, we must leave our baggage behind. What is that baggage?

Our boastful perception of ourselves, our confidence in our own talents, skills, or capabilities is a baggage that hinders us from walking the straight path. Some people think that their confidence in their own capabilities can bring them to an advantageous side, but the fact is, it doesn't. In fact, the more you introspect your worldly perception of yourself, the more you carry that baggage that hinders you from walking the path of becoming a nifty neighbor. Our boastful perception of ourselves is a wall that divides rather than unites.

When we start to shatter that wall every day, we begin to see clearly that we are more common than different. This is the first step to becoming a nifty neighbor. The initial step is to think less of yourself and think more of others.

Donning the *sweater and sneakers* also teaches us to leave those titles and accolades and societal status we may have. We are taught to be welcoming to others just like our nifty neighbors, Mister Rogers and Jesus Christ. The great advantage when we don *our life sweaters and sneakers* is that we no longer need to try so hard to attract people. People are naturally magnetized to real, raw, and humble people without trying. This results in becoming one with others, regardless of who they are. We become more open to people of color, people of opposing views, and people of different nationalities and religions. We begin to co-exist. When we all start to humble ourselves and think that we are all equal – *that no one is above another* – we automatically begin to transform our mental and spiritual viewpoints.

Have you ever been in a situation where you just don't feel like being friends with someone? We feel awkward or worse, we tend to pre-judge a person based on their background or personality, color, or disposition in life. Have we thought too highly of ourselves that we no longer enjoin the helpless, distraught, and needy?

Whatever makes us feel awkward in inviting people to talk to us, or welcoming people to a neighborhood, organization, or group, there is one great lesson that we can get from the opening song of Mister Rogers' Neighborhood. In that song, as we verbally encourage them to be a friend, we are taught to don *our own sweaters and sneakers* at the same time. Let us leave our personal perception of ourselves. Let us start to don the perception that we are all the same, equal, children of God.

When you take the step to wear that humility, you are on your way to becoming a nifty neighbor.

So, before we flip to the next chapter, let us learn to shake off whatever we know of ourselves: our background, profession, belief, status, and worldly perception of ourselves. Together, let us open our doors and borrow the words from Mister Rogers:

Won't you please be my neighbor?

CHAPTER THREE
Nifty Neighbor Character: The Good Samaritan

"You have heard that it was said, 'Love your friends, hate your enemies.' But now I tell you: love your enemies and pray for those who persecute you."

In our quest to find the perfect character of a nifty neighbor, we look at the many stories of the goodness of humanity. After all, a nifty neighbor is someone who possesses compassion for his fellow humans.

We don't have to go too far: our modern-day heroes such as our military men and women who fight against the forces of evil to defend our country are our nifty neighbors, too. Those doctors and nurses who risked their lives to help us recover from the COVID-19 pandemic, displayed amazing heroism, and are considered nifty neighbors.

During the recent pandemic, we witnessed the nifty neighbor character within us during a difficult time – we see people helping people, saving lives, and fighting together. We saw humanity at work during the worst times of the world. Yes, we have lost many lives because of COVID-19, but we certainly saw the display of humanity in each of us. Truly, a remarkable time.

The Good Samaritan

There are so many stories that talk about the goodness of humanity. As I've said, we've seen and heard these stories ourselves. But in the history of this world, there is a great story often retold.

From one generation to another, it set a standard of neighborly love and became the ultimate, inspiring model of the goodness of humanity. That story, shared in the Bible, is the parable of the Good Samaritan – a touching story of a man who extended his helping hand to another man despite their difference in religion.

Before we go deep into this story, let us acknowledge a few of the basic facts during the time of Jesus so that we gain a better interpretation of this timeless piece of narration. It is my hope that we see this story from a different angle, beyond its story of compassion and humanity.

Jesus started to narrate this story when He was giving an example of how we should love others, even those who may not be our friends. In Matthew 5:43-47, Jesus spoke to His disciples: "*You have heard that it was said, 'Love your friends, hate your enemies.' But now I tell you: love your enemies and pray for those who persecute you.*" Jesus also said, *"Love your neighbor as yourself"*.

Confused, His disciples confirmed what he meant by the word "neighbor". This is when he told the Parable of the Good Samaritan (written in Luke 10:25-37), to explain that people should love *everyone*, including their enemies. Jesus explained that it is easy to love friends and family, but it is much more difficult to love those whom you may not get along with or even those who may harm or hurt you. Jesus taught to show love to your enemies meant truly loving the same way Christ did.

And so, Jesus narrated the story of the Good Samaritan which then shattered the cultural ways during those times. How did this story shake the cultural ways of Jesus' time?

The Samaritans and Other Beliefs

We should understand that *Samaritans* are a group of people from Samaria. Samaritan tradition claims that the group descends from the northern Israelite tribes who were not deported by the Neo-Assyrian Empire after the destruction of the Kingdom of Israel. Samaritans believe that they are the true religion of the ancient Israelites and regard Judaism as a closely related but altered religion.

Figure 3: Modern-day Samaritans. Taken in Nablus, Israel - October 4, 2017: Samaritans praying at Mount Gerizim during Sukkot holiday

During those times, the belief systems were so diverse and somewhat stiff that one is identified not by his physical attributes or race, but by religious beliefs. Religion has strongly divided people – between Jews and Samarians, and other religious sects. As written in Brittanica.com, in Jewish Palestine, for example, there were three small but important religious parties that differed from each other in several ways: the Pharisees (numbering about 6,000 at the time of Herod), Essenes (about 4,000), and Sadducees ("a few men," according to Flavius Josephus, in *The Antiquities of the Jews* 18.17). A largely lay group that had the reputation of being the most- precise interpreters of the law, the Pharisees, believed in the resurrection of the dead. They also relied on the nonbiblical "traditions of the fathers," some of which made the law stricter while others relaxed it. The Essenes were a more-radical sect, with extremely strict rules.

These varying religious beliefs about life, death, scriptures, and interpretations of the laws, have sorely divided the nation in Jesus' time. Since every person is identified with his or her religion, you get no help from the "other religions" if you lay on the ground lifeless. So come to think of this: if this story was told at the time of Jesus, then the parable is probably a "weird cast of characters".

Adding to this, the Samaritans, reciprocally, hated the Jews. In fact, tensions between them were particularly high in the early decades of the 1st century because Samaritans had desecrated the Jewish Temple at Passover with human bones.

Knowing all these, I look at Samaritans and Jews like opposing elements in a scientific laboratory that when mixed, surely explode.

Or have you ever watched a movie with confusing characters and things just don't mix up? You finish watching the whole movie and realized, this can't happen in real life. It's just absurd. And with those confusing characters involved in the story, surely, His disciples think the same way.

A Samaritan helping a Jew is unlikely! Because a person that lies helpless and half-dead on the ground will merit assistance only when their cultural or religious backgrounds are parallel.

But Jesus gave a fresh, riveting, and powerful parable that strike the norms. It created a revolutionized perspective on culture that time. A simple story that changed the world forever.

The Parable of the Good Samaritan

In the Parable of the Good Samaritan, Jesus uses the example of the Jew and the Samaritan, who would not ordinarily have been friendly toward each other. They have clashing religious beliefs and are considered mortal enemies. However, out of all those who could have helped the Jew, only the Samaritan did.

Jesus narrates that a man was traveling from Jerusalem to Jericho. He was attacked by robbers on the way and was badly beaten and left half dead on the road. The first person to pass the seemingly lifeless man was a priest, who crossed the road, saw the man's body but continued walking.

A Levite was the second person to pass, who was a priest's assistant. The Levite also crossed the road but did not help the man, instead, continued walking.

Until a Samaritan was the last person to pass by. But when the Samaritan saw the man, he took pity on him. Right there, he bandaged him and cleaned his wounds. The Samaritan put him on the back of his donkey and took him to an innkeeper, whom he paid to look after him. The Samaritan told the innkeeper to watch over him and that he will come back after two days.

Figure 2: A illustration depicting the parable of the good Samaritan.

The parable ends with Jesus giving a commandment to go out and do the same as the Samaritan had done.

It is, however, unique to think that out of all the characters that Jesus could have used in telling this story, He intentionally used religious characters – Samaritans and Jews. We should also note that Levites are male Jews who are members of a group of clans of religious functionaries in ancient Israel who apparently were given a special religious status. Levites at that time, therefore, hold special treatment in their religious society.

Turning Hate to Love

The first glaring lesson of this parable needs no long explanation: *Love your neighbors as yourself.* When we see someone who needs help, Jesus taught us to see ourselves in them or put ourselves in someone's shoes. That is the true mark of a good neighbor.

But seeing ourselves in other people's lives is a difficult thing to do, especially when we are divided. How can we see ourselves in other people's lives if their beliefs or statuses contrast our own?

In your daily life, have you dealt with a situation where you choose to be apathetic than care to avoid judgment or argument? It's like seeing a person whom you know hated you, so you just turn a blind eye and walk out of the situation. But Jesus taught us a different approach in the parable: we must get close to our enemies and become one with them by showing them care, compassion, and ultimately, love.

Yes, they may retaliate or hate us, but Jesus taught this story for it to become a guiding path to harmony – *turn hate to love*. When we learn to extend love to people, perspectives change. And even if we will not be repaid the same, Jesus still commands, "Love your neighbor as yourself."

Break Walls of Religion Through Love

The second glaring lesson of this parable is to break the wall of religious differences and unite as brothers and sisters.

Jesus did not only speak of a certain "man" or "men" in this story. He tagged characters according to their religious affiliation: Jew, Levite, and Samaritan. Jesus intentionally used religious characters to target His mission of allowing people to rethink cultural boundaries, unite religious beliefs, and teach everyone the fact that despite differences, *we are all neighbors.*

During Jesus' time, the religious sects were so concerned with the laws of religion. Punishment is given to those who break religious laws. But when Jesus came, it all shattered the walls that divide humanity. Instead, Jesus focused on the commonality that each human has – LOVE.

This became a reason why Jesus was so hated by the church leaders. They despised Him because of his radical teachings that go against the laws of their churches. Amidst a time of religious hate and persecution, Jesus' teachings tore the walls and finally set free the idea of love, unity, compassion, humanity, and oneness. Jesus knew that He will be hated for His teachings, but He had a mission to illuminate the *light of love* to the world beset by the *dark laws of religion*.

The Actions of the Samaritan

There were four different clever actions that the Samaritan did to the Jew in the parable which we can all learn from in our quest to become nifty neighbors ourselves. Let's elaborate on each one, as we strive to personify the actions of the good Samaritan.

If we look at the parable, there were many levels of actions that truly display a perfect, nifty neighbor.

1. ***He Took Pity / Compassion for the Needy*** – The first verb we can see in the parable from the Samaritan was "pity". The Samaritan *felt* the need to help the Jew who lie lifeless on the ground. This was his initial reaction which prompted him to action. As humans, we all have innate compassion for people who are in helpless situations. However, Jesus taught us *not* to remain in that state of compassion. We must respond to that feeling. The action that we do after that feeling of compassion is what matters to Him. The Samaritan did not only take pity on the plight of the Jew, but he also elevated his compassion into action by doing the necessary steps to help the Jew.

Have we responded in action to the feeling of compassion that we have for our neighbors? Or were we like the Levite who passed by and never showed action to the lifeless Jews?

2. ***Bandaged Him / Care One's Life*** – Considered as the very first action after his feeling of pity, the Samaritan bandaged the Jew. This is an amazing display of care. When one bandages a cut, it is to make sure that the blood does not run out of his body. Therefore, this action by the Samaritan shows that the Samaritan ensured that the Jew would live. By bandaging him, it meant extending life to another life. This action truly magnified the Samaritan's care for his life.

Reflection: Have we met people who are running out of life? They may not necessarily be literally running out of life in a hospital, but they have been too drained to continue with their lives; they feel drained to go on. The parable taught us to extend our helping hand to those whose lifelines are half empty. Our simple touch and care for them could boost their lifelines!

3. **Cleaned His Wounds / Concern and Protecting Life** – We all know that wounds can cause irritation and complications when left unclean. The Samaritan knew there is an impending harm that might cause the Jew hazard to his health which caused the Samaritan the action of cleaning his wounds. This magnifies the concern of the Samaritan for the Jew's life, and his action was to protect him by taking the Jew away from harm.

Reflection: Do we know of someone who is in danger, or in need of our protection? In this action by the Samaritan we are taught to protect those in harm. When we "clean other's wounds" simply by being vigilant to the situations of others, we are taking the first step in protecting our neighbors' lives.

4. **Put Him at the Back of His Donkey / Lending Your Possessions** – Donkeys are a valuable possession for the Samaritans. But in this story, the Samaritan used his prized possession to help the lifeless man. In this action, we are taught that there are possessions that we have in our life that we can use for the benefit of our neighbors. Our "simple things" could be a life source to others. We ought to provide these to our neighbors who badly need them.

   Reflection: Are we keeping important possessions that can help other people in need? Sometimes, our little things could mean the world to some people. It can already create a huge difference in their lives. Let us learn to extend our possessions, no matter how important they are for us, to our neighbors in need.

5. **Took Him to Innkeeper / Giving Time** – From taking pity to bandaging the cuts to cleaning the wounds, the Samaritan did above and beyond what any good man would do. He wasn't finished yet. He took the Jew to the Innkeeper. But there is another lesson we learn from this act of kindness from the Samaritan. Riding his prized, slow-moving donkey to the innkeeper must have required a lot of time and effort. But the Samaritan offered his precious time. In this parable, Jesus taught us not only to lend our possessions but also to lend our precious time.

Reflections: What is our extent of willingness to extend our time for others?

Figure 3: Arrival of the Good Samaritan at the Inn - Picture from the Holy Scriptures, Old and New Testaments books collection published in 1885, Stuttgart-Germany. Drawings by Gustave Dore.

6. ***Paid the Innkeeper / Generosity*** – The Samaritan did not leave the Jew until he is assured of his safety. The Samaritan gives two denarii – approximately two days' wages – to the

innkeeper to pay for any expenses the innkeeper might incur in caring for the man; and he pledges to repay the innkeeper for expenses beyond the two denarii. Imagine this: two days of wages is what the two denarii meant for the Samaritan so apart from the time he spent caring for the Jew and lending his possessions, he sacrificed his two days-worth money for the Jew. Other than this, the Samaritan also pledged to the innkeeper that he will repay him for whatever the innkeeper might incur for caring for the man. This parable magnified the amazing extent of the generosity of the good Samaritan despite their religious difference.

Reflections: Have we shown generosity to the people who are in need of help? Are we willing to pay the innkeeper for our needy enemies to have a better life? Sounds impossible, but truly, this is the kind of love Jesus wants us to reflect and possess.

Be More Like the Good Samaritan, Less of a Levite

In our next discussions, we will use the good Samaritan story as we explore and uncover the various characteristics of a good neighbor. In this part of our exploration, we learn that compassion, selflessness, and breaking differences of beliefs are key to becoming a good neighbor.

This story teaches generations to love their enemies. And when you say love, it is the love that not only cares, but extends to *being compassionate* to them, *protecting* them, *lending* them a *hand*, *giving* them our *time*, and *being generous* to them.

As I discussed in the introduction of this book, we have all been divided because of our religious beliefs, moral standards, political views, etcetera. This generation thirsts for validation and approval from the world. In this parable, however, we are taught to shake those off and let go of what we know of ourselves.

Remember the Levite who passed by and never cared for the Jew? The Levites as we learned have a special religious status. We learn, therefore, that the more we hold tightly to our societal status or worldly titles, we become inclined to care less for those who are in need. Our titles are a stronghold that if we cannot shake off, bars us from becoming a nifty neighbor.

So, let's crash the barriers that divide us and our enemies, and together, let us learn from Jesus' compassion story. That way, we will embody the character of a good Samaritan, the character of a nifty neighbor. So, ask yourself, how can I start to embody the character of the good Samaritan today?

CHAPTER FOUR
Our Television Neighbor, Mister Rogers

""I'm glad we can be together again." - Mister Rogers

There is no show in the world that can possibly match the kind of storytelling creativity done by the famous Fred Rogers. With three long decades in television, he has gained worldwide fame, won four Emmy Awards, and the most prestigious accolades in the television industry. Indeed, *"Mister Rogers' Neighborhood"* is a show that is yet to be contested.

There is a level of delight with a little sensitivity in the show which made it even more interesting to children and families. The program does not only entertain but speaks to children about how to process weighty topics from racism to the assassination of Robert Kennedy. It tackles divorce, death, racial intolerance, and all the other realities that children may face in their lives. This made the show even more interesting as it "prepares the children" to become adults with loads of fun elements!

But there is much to say about the person behind this popular program. The genius behind it is Mister Rogers himself, or Mr. Fred Rogers in real life.

Born Fred McFeely Rogers, Mister Rogers was born on the 20th of March 1928. More fondly called Mister Rogers, he was a television host, author, producer, and Presbyterian minister. Other than hosting the show, he was the founder, showrunner, and host of the show which ran for three decades - from 1968 to 2001.

Rogers was born in Latrobe, Pennsylvania. He earned a bachelor's degree in music from Rollins College in 1951. He graduated from Pittsburgh Theological Seminary with a bachelor's degree in divinity in 1962 and became a Presbyterian minister in 1963. He attended the University of Pittsburgh's Graduate School of Child Development, where he began his 30-year collaboration with child psychologist Margaret McFarland who later became his lifelong mentor and consultant to the show, and whose expertise he carried out in his episodes.

Mister Rogers began his television career at NBC in New York. Aside from *Mister Rogers' Neighborhood*, he also helped develop the children's shows The Children's Corner in 1955 for WQED in Pittsburgh and *Misterogers* in 1963 in Canada for the Canadian Broadcasting Corporation. In 1968, he returned to Pittsburgh and adapted the format of his Canadian series to create *Mister Rogers' Neighborhood.* That is where it all began for Rogers.

Awards and Recognitions

From that time on, the show ran for more than three decades with a total of 33 years. The show garnered awards and recognition for focusing on children's emotional and physical concerns and how it carried out the stories creatively yet gently. The show was applauded for delivering topics that connect to children's lives and their realities – sibling rivalry, school enrollment, divorce, and even death.

Though Rogers passed on due to stomach cancer in 2003, at the age of 74, his legacy lived on. His work in children's television has been widely lauded, and he received more than 40 honorary degrees and several awards, including the Presidential Medal of Freedom in 2002 and a Lifetime Achievement Emmy in 1997. He was inducted into the Television Hall of Fame in 1999.

Aside from this, Rogers influenced many writers and producers of children's television shows, and his broadcasts provided comfort during tragic events, even after his death.

Fred Rogers and His Dedication to Children

Fred Rogers dedicated his life to understanding childhood. He took that knowledge to the medium of television in his groundbreaking series.

Over more than 30 years Mister Rogers cemented a relationship with millions of television viewers – not just children but also families. Each episode felt like Mister Rogers was visiting with a trusted friend. On his website, MisterRogers.org, it says, "Mister Rogers looked directly into the camera and sang and talked to each child watching. His radical kindness, acceptance, and empathy created a place that as TV Guide described: '... makes us, young and old alike, feel safe, cared for and valued... Wherever Mister Rogers is, so is sanctuary.'"

Figure 4: Winter Park, Florida -2022: Mister Rogers with Daniel Tiger and children. "A Beautiful Day for a Neighbor," a 360-degree outdoor sculpture at Rollins College by British sculptor Paul Day, dedicated to Mister Rogers.

Mister Rogers created a safe space for children to enjoy and – most importantly – to learn important values and acceptance of the realities of life, making them ready to face puberty or teenagerhood, and the bigger challenges ahead of them. Mister Rogers made every child feel that they are enough. His famous lines *"There is only one person in the whole world like you, and people can like you just because you're you."*

MisterRogers.org website says, "With that kind of encouragement, we could manage our fears and feelings, and be willing to try new things even if we might fail. His support helped us to become competent, compassionate, and caring adults."

The Message of Mister Rogers

The core message of Mister Rogers can be seen in each of his episodes through his discussions, stories, songs, and rhymes. He had a complete package full of interesting ideas and lessons for children to receive and live by. But what is the core message of the show?

On his website, MisterRogers.org, we see the various messages that he intended to deliver:

1. **He makes us feel good about who we are** - Mister Rogers made us feel valued and loved. "*There is only one person in the whole world like you, and people can like you just because you're you.*" With that kind of encouragement, we could manage our fears and feelings, and be willing to try new things even if we might fail. His support helped us to become competent, compassionate, and caring adults.

Figure 5: Mister Rogers' statue in Pittsburg, Pennsylvania

2. **He helps us with our feelings** - Mister Rogers helped children understand that feelings – all kinds of feelings – are natural and normal. Feelings are a part of being human. He encouraged us to talk about our feelings so that we could manage them, because *"Whatever is mentionable can be more manageable."* And he showed us some of the many ways people express their feelings.
3. **He helps us with our relationship with others** - In Mister Rogers' Neighborhood, everyone was welcomed and valued. Mister Rogers helped us appreciate and respect others. He opened his door to all and warmly invited them to share their talents and ideas. He showed us the power of kindness and compassion, "You are special and so is everyone else in this world."
4. **He helps us wonder and learn** - Mister Rogers gave us the tools to be lifelong learners – a sense of wonder, a curiosity about the world around us, and the willingness to ask questions. His genuine interest in the world was infectious. Whatever he showed us, he encouraged us to look and listen carefully, to keep trying, and to see the world as a wondrous place. *"Did you know when you wonder, you're learning."*

Figure 5: Mister Rogers' star on the Hollywood Walk of Fame.

5. **He helps us be ready for new experiences** - *"I like to be told,"* Mister Rogers sang. He understood that new experiences or changes in routine can feel overwhelming and scary to young children. He showed us what to expect. He reassured us. He prepared us to meet and trust the people who would care for us – the doctor, the dentist, the barber, the teacher.

6. **He talks to us honestly about difficult subjects** - Mister Rogers was not afraid to tackle tough subjects. From divorce, to assassination, to death, he talked honestly and openly about subjects that adults were often afraid to talk about, but which children often silently wondered and worried about. And he was willing to help children, and adults too, know that there are some things no one can understand. *"Some things I don't understand."*

With the great messages from Mister Rogers and how he cemented his place in the hearts of children (who are now adults), he was able to share the goodness of his heart and made the lives of millions of children better and easier.

A mark of a good and nifty neighbor is the ability to change other people's lives. Indeed, Mister Rogers did not only bring entertainment that stuck to our minds and hearts, he changed them.

CHAPTER FIVE
12 Good Neighbor Lessons from Mister Rogers

In the previous chapter, we learned about the contribution of our nifty neighbor, Mister Rogers to child development globally. His expertise in communicating to children effectively through creative and impactful ways serves as a standard for generations of TV shows and child development programs. Each topic he exposed – the fun, sensitive, yet relatable portions – in all of his episodes brought eye-opening perspectives to the young mind.

Mister Rogers perfectly blended the important physical, mental, spiritual, and emotional factors in his stories – softly, gently, and maturely. His creative techniques of storytelling are still unparalleled up to this day. And with his 30 years of experience, dissecting his ways and attempting to summarize it all is close to impossibility. There were just too many beautiful pieces of advice and lessons that everyone can pick up in Mister Rogers' Neighborhood. And Mister Rogers' Neighborhood, being a masterpiece at that, is one that hard to replicate.

The 12 Good Neighbor Lessons

But in this chapter, we still strive to still uncover how the masterpiece is made, and what elements make the show and Mister Rogers himself the finest pair of all.

Here are the 12 Good Neighbor Lessons that I believe are important chunks from the large serving that are surely worth noting. This is just *a tip of the iceberg,* but I believe that these somehow perfectly summarize the positive impacts of Mister Rogers in our lives that elevated him to become the most unforgettable television neighbor in the world.

I adopted the article here as written by Kelly Bryant and published on the page ReadersDigest.com:

1. Conflict is a natural part of the community

Fred Rogers didn't try to pretend as though bringing a diverse group of people together in one neighborhood was easy. In fact, from the get-go *Mister Rogers' Neighborhood* addressed differing opinions, as noted in the documentary *Won't You Be My Neighbor?*. When King Friday XIII responds to changes in the Neighborhood of Make-Believe by putting up a barbed wire wall, the neighborhood reaches out with peaceful concern. Coming from a place of compassionate worry, the two sides are able to come to a mutually beneficial solution.

2. Yes, people with different beliefs can co-exist

Mister Rogers often used his character King Friday as an example of someone whose strong beliefs, fears, and sometimes unsettling actions could still be met with peaceable communication. In one instance, the other members of the Neighborhood of Make-Believe sent the frustrated king balloon messages bearing their own concerns and wishes. When one side attempted to understand where the other was coming from, calm resolutions could be achieved.

3. Remind friends of their authentic value

Mister Rogers always closed his show reminding the audience, "I like you as you are." It was an important message to send to children, who may often feel like they are different or less than their peers and grownups. Instead of harping on what they could change to be a "better" person, the sweater-wearing TV icon communicated a sense of peace and loving oneself as they are at that very moment. Instilling this sense of confidence in children and loved ones is just as important today.

4. Love your neighbor and love yourself

Despite his background as a Presbyterian minister, Mister Rogers didn't try to push a specific agenda on his viewers. Instead, he was a glorious example of someone who could be open to hearing other people's opinions without diverting from his own values. This characteristic is surely something the world could benefit from practicing today. Listening to the other "side" doesn't mean you have to give up on what you believe, it simply makes your world more diverse.

5. Be a good listener

Mister Rogers didn't preach good listening skills in the typical sense, which to many could mean just being quiet so someone else can share information or speak their peace. Instead, he encouraged truly paying attention to what another person is saying. Listening with not only your ears, but your eyes, heart, and soul. Words mean very little if we're not open to understanding the feelings and thoughts behind them.

6. We respond best when there's an attempt to understand

The television host was all about making heartfelt attempts to understand a differing opinion before uttering a response. He felt that the very act of learning what someone's feelings are grounded in can make others react with an increased sense of care and rationale. In today's world of social media retorts and arguments, there's never been a better time to practice this lesson.

7. Treat everyone with respect

This lesson might feel like a no-brainer, the kind of thing any child learns in kindergarten. But Rogers didn't only say the words, he also illustrated the point visually. During a time when black people weren't allowed to swim in the same pools as white folks, the Pittsburgh, PA native wanted to make a point against this segregation. He invited series regular Officer Clemmons, played by African-American actor Francois Scarborough Clemmons, to cool his feet alongside him in a kiddie pool during a segment. We're all in this great, big, crazy world together.

"When I was a boy and I would see scary things in the news, my mother would say to me, 'Look for the helpers. You will always find people who are helping,'" said Mister Rogers. He held that conversation close to his heart until his passing in 2003, resting peacefully in the knowledge that there are still caring people ready to help. When considering your place in the community, be a helper.

8. Don't be afraid to discuss the tough stuff

After taking a brief absence from children's television, Mister Rogers came back in the 1980s with a series of shows that tackled serious issues for kids. He discussed heavy topics like death and divorce but did so in a relatable way that wasn't condescending. Mister Rogers opened up the lines of communication for kids who may not otherwise have had an outlet for such conversations. Today, with children facing a multitude of outside challenges, it's helpful to remember that their innate emotions and feelings are just as curious and delicate as ever before.

9. Build people up

Mister Rogers was a big proponent of instilling confidence in people, pointing out their greatest assets as opposed to critiquing their weaknesses. He could find a point of understanding in just about everyone. "I think those who try to make you feel less than you are—that's the greatest evil," he said in an interview that appeared in *Won't You Be My Neighbor?*. Find a connection and offer support to neighbors, with the hope that they will return this in kind.

10. Expect and accept mistakes

No one is perfect, not even the seemingly wonderful Mister Rogers. He was very much aware of this, which is why one of his greatest lessons to viewers was to expect and accept mistakes. By doing so we not only learn to be less hard on ourselves but others as well. Embracing imperfections is a simple way to make more out of life.

11. What is essential in life is invisible to the eye

During a public speaking engagement, Rogers paraphrased a popular quote from *The Little Prince*—that what is essential in life is invisible to the eye. "What changes the world?" he asked. "The only thing that really changes the world is when somebody gets the idea that love can abound and can be shared."

12. Take time to think about someone who has helped you

During a typical harried day, we may off-handedly thank those around us for their helping hand or a kind word. During his speaking engagements, Mister Rogers often asked his audience to take one full minute to think about someone who has really helped them in life. Doing so might bring a tear to their eye, a smile to their face, or warmth to their heart. Adding this simple practice to everyday life not only makes us a better neighbor—and a more grateful person as well.

CHAPTER SIX
Jesus Christ

Jesus Christ *(from the Hebrew name Yeshua)* was born between 4 BC and 6 BC or roughly around 2000 years ago. He is the most popular personality who ever walked the face of this planet because of his indelible mark on the belief system of the world.

Unlike the kings and lords of the old times, our good and nifty neighbor, Jesus Christ trod a path of humble beginnings. Born from a manger, the poorest possible place where one could be born (A manger or trough is a rack for fodder, or a structure or feeder used to hold food for animals); born in a town almost unknown to many – Jesus was, without question, came from the poor and ordinary. Historians believe that Jesus spent the unrecorded years of His life in His hometown, working with His dad as a carpenter.

Figure 6: Birth of Jesus – painting illustration from Milan Church, Milan, Italy.

Early Years of Jesus

Jesus began his ministry when he was around 30 years old. But even as a child, His parents knew there was something special about Him. He possesses a different level of maturity and intelligence. As written in Luke 2:41-45 (NIV):

Every year Jesus' parents went to Jerusalem for the Festival of the Passover. When he was twelve years old, they went up to the festival, according to the custom. After the festival was over, while his parents were returning home, the boy Jesus stayed behind in Jerusalem, but they were unaware of it. Thinking he was in their company, they traveled on for a day. Then they began looking for him among their relatives and friends. When they did not find him, they went back to Jerusalem to look for him. After three days they found him in the temple courts, sitting among the teachers, listening to them and asking them questions. Everyone who heard him was amazed at his understanding and his answers. When his parents saw him, they were astonished. His mother said to him, "Son, why have you treated us like this? Your father and I have been anxiously searching for you."

"Why were you searching for me?" he asked. "Didn't you know I had to be in my Father's house?" But they did not understand what he was saying to them.

Then he went down to Nazareth with them and was obedient to them. But his mother treasured all these things in her heart. And Jesus grew in wisdom and stature, and in favor with God and man.

Jesus' Start of Ministry

Jesus founded His own core group of 12 disciples composed of tax collectors and fishermen. His disciples namely; Peter, Andrew, James, John, Philip, Bartholomew/Nathanael, Matthew, Thomas, James son of Alphaeus, Simon the Zealot, Judas the Greater, and Judas Iscariot are names that have been closely associated with Jesus' teaching since the earliest days of Christianity.

His set of disciples, as I mentioned in my other book "Consummate Coaches," Jesus, knew the risks involved when he coached his disciples. First, he knew that he will be ridiculed for his selection of his own "team" – composed of fishermen, a tax collector, and some activists. The people wouldn't believe him because of his choice of disciples. Choosing his disciples alone was a risk.

In the Bible, Jesus took the risk for the forgiveness of sins. When Jesus started to preach the gospel, people were mad at him and wanted him to be thrown off the cliff. It is written in Luke 4:29: They rose up, drove him out of the town, and led him to the brow of the hill on which their town had been built, to hurl him down headlong.

Radical Movement of Christ

During Jesus' time, religious laws were stiff and strict. There is less room for freedom of religious expression. According to *Brittanica.com*, Judaism, as the Jewish religion came to be known in the 1st century CE, and was based on ancient Israelite religion, shown of many of its Canaanite characteristics but with the addition of important features from Babylonia and Persia.

The Jews differed from other people in the ancient world because they believed that there was only one God. Like other people, they worshipped their God with animal sacrifices offered at a temple. The Jews also believed that they had been specially chosen by the one God of the universe to serve him and obey his laws. Although set apart from other people, they believed God called on them to be a "light to the Gentiles" and lead them to accept the God of Israel as the only God.

The Pharisees, a Jewish social movement during the time of Jesus, were known as the "separated ones." Pharisees follow a strict avoidance of gentiles, persons considered unclean, sinners, and Jews who are less observant of the law. Laws were very much important to the Pharisees.

The Pharisees aim to extend the practice of their religion to the everyday lives of people. They were motivated by a zeal for Judaism.

The basis of their teaching was not only the written law (called Torah) and the prophets but also various oral traditions of detailed observances and practices which they themselves inherited.

The positive aspects of the work of the Pharisees were: they extended the practice of religion beyond the temple, into the lives of ordinary people; and they wished to remind people of the presence of God among them and to call them to respond to his presence by observing certain religious practices.

No wonder that when Jesus performed his miracles and spread his parables and teachings, the religious leaders thought it to be blasphemy and a violation of the religious laws. Jesus' teachings and actions were radical. Jesus cared for the sick, dined with the sinners, and talked to a tax collector, the adulteress, and the prostitutes. He was one with the unclean and the judged groups of people.

Therefore, Jesus' ways and teachings seemed to have sparked a radical movement in His time. He was shifting the course of religion by teaching God's word, but allowing forgiveness and mercy anchored on love. His teachings became what we often call today a *"viral" content* as news spread from town to town, continuously raising the eyebrows of religious leaders who felt threatened by his popularity.

Figure 7: 17th Century painted illustration of Jesus Christ at the age of 12 teaching in the temple. Painting displayed at St. Nicholas Church, Brussels, Belgium.

While Jesus humbled himself and sat down with the poor and the sick, the Pharisees exerted a great influence on other Jews through their piety and learning. To some extent, the Pharisees showed nationalist and racist attitudes towards foreigners, while Jesus welcomed every race, belief, and background with open arms. While Pharisees kept alive a certain sense of national and religious identity, Jesus only cared for a few important things – to heal the sick, to forgive the sinners, and to spread the news of God's power and mercy.

While the Pharisees believe that there was no hope for other people who were deprived of the law, our nifty neighbor Jesus taught that there is hope for everyone who believes in the Son of God. And while Pharisees believe that only the righteous in Israel could have a share in the world to come, Jesus taught that the eternal life is everyone through the grace of Christ.

Christianity Today

Fast-forward to today, Jesus now has two billion followers, while Christianity, Jesus' founded religion/belief, is still the biggest religion on the planet. According to Lifeway Research, not only is religion growing overall, but Christianity specifically is growing. With a 1.17% growth rate, almost 2.56 billion people will identify as a Christian by the middle of 2022. With this upward trend, by 2050, that number is expected to top 3.33 billion.

Undeniably, Christianity is the largest and biggest religion or belief in the world. If Mister Rogers has the program *"Mister Rogers' Neighborhood,"* our other nifty neighbor Jesus Christ has the Bible, a compilation of stories written by anointed people, who documented his life and teachings.

The Bible, considered the guiding literature for Christians, is the largest-selling book of all time. *Wordsrated.com* compiled the most accurate Bible statistics that bring us to an estimate as to how large the influence is of Christianity today:

The Bible makes up a large portion of religious book sales and revenue. In order to better understand its place in the book market, we researched, analyzed, and collected 32 bible sales statistics covering everything from how many Bibles are sold, how many Bibles are printed, and more.

How many Bibles are printed every year?

- On average, there are 100 million Bibles printed each year.
- It's projected that there are more than 6 billion Bibles currently in print – 140% more than the estimated 2.5 billion copies in print as of 1975.

How many Bibles are sold per year?

- The number of Bibles sold on average has more than doubled in the US since 1950 with:

  - 20 million Bibles sold each year
  - 1.66 million Bibles sold each month
  - 384,615 Bibles sold per week
  - 54,945 Bibles sold every day
  - 2,289 Bibles sold per hour
  - 38 Bibles sold per minute
  - 6.4 Bibles sold every 10 seconds

- In addition to the Bibles sold, another 115,055 Bibles are given away or distributed every day.
- The US accounts for a quarter of newly printed Bible sales every year.

Bible sales revenue per year

- Bible sales revenue per year is approximately $430 million as of 2020
- In the world today, there are more than 80,000 different versions of the Bible that generate at least 1 sale annually.

Bible sales by publisher

- Gideon's sold and distributed approximately 100 bibles per minute, or 59.5 million, in 2016
- The Good News version of the bible sold 18 million copies alone in 1995
- The Bible publisher Thomas Nelson sold for $473 million in 2005
- One Bible publisher, Zondervan, lists nearly 400 versions of the Bible as being in print and for sale

How many books are in the Bible?

- There are 66 books in the protestant Bible.
- These are split in a number of ways, but the major differentiation is between the old testament and the new testament.
- The old testament deals with life before the birth of Jesus and prophecies of his coming.
- The new testament deals with the birth, life, and death of Jesus.
- There are 39 books in the old testament.
- There are 27 books in the new testament — broken down into the letters of church leaders and the 4 gospels of Matthew, Make, Luke, and John.
- There are 1,189 chapters and 31,173 verses in The Bible.
- In the Catholic Bible, there are 73 books — 46 in the old testament and 27 in the new testament.

Without the need for accolades or awards, there is no denying, that based on the statistics or figures above, the Bible's popularity, distribution, and worldwide presence (it is the most translated book of all time, too!) no book could surpass its record, ever.

Teachings of Jesus

The teachings of Jesus remain relevant these days. In fact, in our daily lives, His teachings continue to govern the land. It served as the foundation of the laws of the United States of America. I wrote this in my first book, *"Extreme Entrepreneurs: Steve Jobs and Jesus Christ"* (you may check out Amazon.com to avail of the book).

"The rebel, Jesus Christ, started a revolution among humans that took almost eighteen hundred years to become the foundation for governing the people of the United States. His influence is global, but the only governing body that is based on his person- centric teachings is the United States. Today, there are estimated to be about 70 percent of the US population that has some soul connection to Jesus Christ, by identifying as Christians.

Jesus, the individual, lived as he taught. Jesus, the messenger of God, put the individual in the center of life and asks that each person must "love your neighbor as yourself."

Jesus' ever-relevant and timeless teachings not only serve as the foundation of laws but also acts as a guiding principle to creating future laws. The harmony of humanity that Christ laid out in His blueprint, the Bible, is a living Word that brings societies a certain level of order.

When love becomes our guide, there is life.

An American author, educator, and speaker Stephen Covey says, "Live the law of Love. We encourage obedience to laws of life when we live the laws of love."

CHAPTER SEVEN
The Neighbor in the Bible

"You shall love your neighbor as yourself." – Romans 13:10

Now that we have a better perspective on what a nifty neighbor is from the stories of Mister Rogers, let us look at the other spectrum to get the full 360-degree view. In this chapter, I'd like us to dive deep into what the Bible has to say about a neighbor. We answer the questions: Who are considered nifty neighbors - biblically? From a spiritual standpoint, how do we become nifty neighbors?

As we strive to uncover the answers, let's look at the Bible, Jesus Christ's message to the world.

If Mister Rogers communicates his ideas and perspectives through his thought-provoking and award-winning program, *"Mister Rogers' Neighborhood,"* then our other nifty neighbor, Jesus, communicates through the Bible, the best-selling book of all time. It is, as we learned previously, the most translated book in the world and the bestseller of bestsellers. Given this mind-blowing and unparalleled record of the Bible, we find it important to also see what the Bible has to say about being a nifty neighbor. This is because the Bible, even though it provides almost a similar definition to those previous definitions we studied, still has a different point-of-view (millennials and Gen Zs often call it POV in social media, by the way, which I will use in the coming chapters).

By the end of this chapter, we discover that the Bible provides the world with different, unique, and comprehensive meanings of a *neighbor*, by referencing "self". Let's uncover.

Like *Mister Rogers' Neighborhood*, the Bible also tackles sensitive topics that are written in straightforward language. Most importantly, the Bible brings eye-opening messages about *becoming a neighbor* that serves as a guiding path for life. Like Fred Rogers' program, the Bible also prepares us for the life ahead – giving us the tips and tricks to handle different situations from a spiritual standpoint.

Here, let's open our hearts, and together, let us get a clear picture of Jesus' POV of a nifty neighbor.

The Neighbor in the Word

It is worth noting that the word "neighbor" was mentioned in 163 instances in the Bible. Imagine – *one hundred and sixty-three times*! Indeed, the Bible has so much to say about a neighbor making clear that our nifty neighbor, Jesus, really made a great deal of time in emphasizing the importance of *being a nifty neighbor* in the gospel. In His preaching, what does He say about a neighbor?

Romans 13:8-10 and Mark 12:30-31 encapsulate it all. These verses give us a quick and short yet profound idea of what the biblical neighbor is. These verses will also be our main focus of discussion.

In Romans 13:8-10 (NIV):

(8) Let no debt remain outstanding, except the continuing debt to love one another, for whoever loves others has fulfilled the law.

(9) "For the commandments, 'You shall not commit adultery, You shall not murder, You shall not steal, You shall not covet,' and any other commandment, are summed up in this word: 'You shall love your neighbor as yourself.'

(10) Love does no wrong to a neighbor; therefore, love is the fulfillment of the law.

In Mark 12:30-31 (NIV):

(30) "'You shall love the Lord your God with all your heart, and with all your soul, and with all your mind, and with all your strength. '

(31) The second is this, 'You shall love your neighbor as yourself. ' There is no other commandment greater than these."

Learning this from the New Testament, *"loving thy neighbor"* therefore, is a pathway for the fulfillment of all of God's commandments, according to Jesus. In simple terms, it is the ingredient to all ingredients, not just the icing on a cake. It is the fulfillment of the law.

I also see this in a different way: In college, we learned about subject prerequisites. It taught us that to make sense of the study of trigonometry, we first must be adept with algebra and geometry. But to make sense of algebra, we need fluency in basic math: addition, subtraction, multiplication, and division. The same notion applies to the rule of *loving thy neighbor.* You must learn to love your neighbor as yourself because this golden rule will elevate you to follow each of the commandments written in the Old Testament.

What are those commandments? In Romans 13:8-10, Jesus made mention some of the commandments, but I'd like us to interpret the commandments one by one, in our effort to realize how *"loving thy neighbor"* is fundamental to fulfilling each of them, and why *"loving thy neighbor"* is one of the two greatest commandments.

The 10 Commandments and a Nifty Neighbor

If you grew up as a Christian, perhaps you memorized these Ten Commandments, written in Exodus 20: 3-17. As a background, this came about when God chose Moses to deliver His people from the bondage of slavery in Egypt by parting the Red Sea so the Israelites could cross to freedom.

Moses then led the Israelites to Mount Sinai where God gave Moses the Ten Commandments, as well as the other laws for right living. He also provided the blueprint for building a Tabernacle. At that time, God was forming a Holy Nation prepared to live for and serve Him (which disappointed Moses because when he came back from the mountain, he saw the people worshipping idols, which caused the tablets to fall from his hands and break).

The 10 commandments read:

1. You shall have no other Gods before me.
2. Thou shalt not make unto thee any graven images.
3. Thou shalt not take the name of the Lord thy God in vain.

These first three laws were very important. The Israelites needed them to become a strong nation amidst some groups of people worshipping idols. Fulfilling these first two laws is pledging allegiance to be loyal and obedient to the One God.

We don't like it if people call us bad names, do we? It shows disrespect. This commandment reminds us that God's name is Holy, and it must be used only in a reverent way.

Some people take God's name in vain because others are doing it and we find ourselves saying these words that dishonor God. It can take root in our hearts and mind and begin saying it and don't realize we did.

These first commandments talk about the relationship of humans to God (not humans to neighbors), as mentioned in the first great commandment: *'You shall love the Lord your God with all your heart, and with all your soul, and with all your mind, and with all your strength.'*

4. Remember the Sabbath day and keep it Holy.

Back in the Old Testament, this meant they should not work on the Sabbath but they carried it too far and wouldn't let people pick up something heavy. Jesus changed this and said we should keep the Sabbath day to worship, remember creation, and rest so we could serve God and others. This part of the commandments combines the two great commandments together. When we remember Sabbath, it is a display of love for God. When we keep it Holy by serving others, it is a display of love for our neighbors.

5. Honor your father and mother.

Honoring means loving and respecting. When one honors his parents, it is a symbol of love and respect. God wanted homes to be happy, so He made this an important rule. Respect is a character of a nifty neighbor.

6. Thou shalt not kill.

God cares for each human life. When one loves his neighbor as his self, it translates that he cares for the safety of the life of his neighbor, too. Concern for life is a character of a nifty neighbor.

7. Thou shalt not commit adultery.

This means husbands and wives should be faithful to one another. Adultery has broken many families, thus, when one truly loves his neighbor, one is naturally faithful to his partner. Faithfulness is a character of a nifty neighbor.

8. Thou shalt not steal.

No one is permitted to take something that belongs to another. Not only is it God's law but it is the basic law of the society we live in. There are material things that we value so much in this world. If we love our neighbor like ourselves, we learn to feel what others feel when they lose their important possessions. This commandment magnified empathy as an important characteristic of a nifty neighbor.

9. Thou shall not bear false witness.

The commandments warn us of lying or bearing false witness about our neighbors. Telling false stories about our neighbors inflict pain on another. When we truly love our neighbor, we learn to speak only the truth about them even if it puts us at a disadvantage. Truthfulness is a characteristic of a nifty neighbor.

10. You shall not covet your neighbor's house.

Covet means to want something that belongs to someone else. A person who covets may be led to break all most all the other commandments. Loving thy neighbor like ourselves means being happy at the happiness of others — their success or accomplishments.

The Summary Commandment

All these commandments, according to Jesus can be summed up to two of the greatest commandments: (1) *Love God with your heart, mind, soul, and strength;* (2) *Love your Neighbor as yourself.* In these two commandments, the commonality is love — love for

God and love for neighbors.

This *"Great Commandment Concept"* will innately bring spiritual wisdom and strength to keep the 10 commandments to heart.

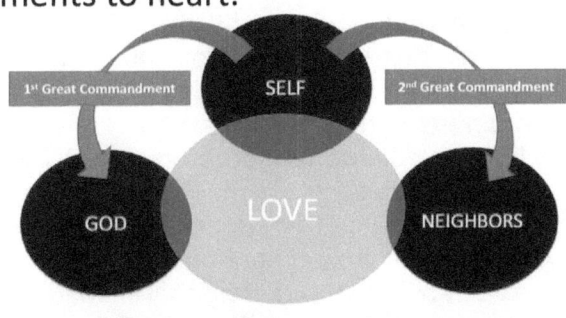

Figure 7. The Great Commandment Concept shows "love for God" and "love for neighbors" as its foundations, anchored on love.

Therefore, loving your neighbor as a starting point will naturally provide us the spiritual resistance to not coveting others' belongings, not bearing false witness, not stealing, not committing adultery, and not killing. When we love our neighbors, we also learn to love our parents. Thus, the power of the commandment *"Loving thy neighbor"* possesses the ability that encompasses the other commandments, a fundamental to obedience – a guiding light that results in the fulfillment of the commandments set by God.

Love and Neighbor

Let us remember the important element that is adjoined by the word neighbor in this great commandment (as shown in the Great Commandment Concept Diagram) – and that is *love*. Love and Neighbor were the two most powerful words in this commandment, that when adjoined, bring a powerful message and will then define what a nifty neighbor is.

Jesus, throughout His life, spoke about love more than anything else. Love was the very core of His messages. In fact, he was hated for it which resulted in his death on the cross. What caused the hate? It was the same love that made him dine with the sinners, the adulterers, the thieves, and the most hated people in society. All these, because of love.

Jesus said, "It is not the healthy who need a doctor, but the sick. But go and learn what this means: `I desire mercy, not sacrifice. ' For I have not come to call the righteous, but sinners."

Remember that we learned how stiff the religious laws were as discussed in the previous chapters. Religious laws established a division amongst people – the holy and unholy, the righteous and sinners, the lawbreakers versus the "clean."

Adding insult to injury, Jesus taught the gospel by example which angered the religious leaders: Jesus showed that loving your neighbor is not just loving a certain group of people. It is inclusive. It is not choosing to love the holy neighbors alone, but extending it to loving the unlovable, spiritually sick neighbors. Jesus taught that we should love the *unclean neighbors, the unrighteous neighbors, the hateful neighbors, the unjust neighbors, and the unholy neighbors.* Jesus' teaching was to open our arms and embrace those who have sinned and fallen short of the glory of God - because we all have fallen short. Not a single one is spiritually clean.

In Romans 3:23, Jesus taught, "For all have sinned and fall short of the glory of God." Self-righteousness or societal status does not make one any closer to God's glory.

Nifty Neighbor Character: The Story of Mary Magdalene

This same love was what Jesus showed when Mary Magdalene was persecuted by her neighbors. John 8 narrates this story:

"The teachers of the law and the Pharisees brought in a woman caught in adultery. They made her stand before the group and said to Jesus, 'Teacher, this woman was caught in the act of adultery.' In the Law, Moses commanded us to stone such women. Now, what do you say?' They were using this question as a trap to have a basis for accusing him.

But Jesus bent down and started to write on the ground with his finger. When they kept on questioning him, he straightened up and said to them, 'If any one of you is without sin, let him be the first to throw a stone at her.' Again he stooped down and wrote on the ground.

At this, those who heard began to go away one at a time, the older ones first, until only Jesus was left, with the woman still standing there. Jesus straightened up and asked her, 'Woman, where are they? Has no one condemned you?' 'No one, sir,' she said. 'Then neither do I condemn you,' Jesus declared. 'Go now and leave your life of sin.'"

This story reminds me of the kind of neighbor Jesus is. This character of a neighbor is exactly what the Bible wants us to become: a neighbor whose judgment is based *on love, not hate.*

A story from a pastor deeply moved me, and I recall: "If I want to reach the moon, I could attempt to go climb the highest mountain and reach its peak. When I do so, I am higher than you. I could stare down at you and feel closer to the moon than anyone else because I am at a higher place. But no matter how I try to reach the moon, I will never have the ability to grab it by my hands. Because even if I have the highest honor in the world – the riches, the praises, the high status – we both could not reach the moon just the same."

Your place in society does not guarantee you righteousness. You are no closer to God than those unrighteous, poor, and unholy people. This same message is what reverberated in the time of Jesus when He spread the Word, reminding us to be humble and become one with our neighbors – regardless of their past, background, or faith.

Now, let's answer the questions we threw at the beginning of this chapter: who are considered the nifty neighbors based on the standards of the Bible? Based on the words of Jesus, *anyone* can be a nifty neighbor when love becomes a guiding light to every decision and action. Another important angle the Bible teaches us is that the nifty neighbors in this world are those who see other people as equals – regardless of their race, beliefs, and backgrounds.

Like Mister Rogers, who exposed the lessons of racial equality on national television to teach young children that we are all equal, we also need to embody this racial tolerance by heart (or any tolerance to differences, for that matter) towards others and shatter the differences that so often block the way for healthier and better relationships.

How can we possibly embody these characteristics?

Call to Action: Be the Nifty Neighbor

Christian Health Ministries, a non-profit organization based in Ohio, posted this inspiring summary of nifty or good neighbor characteristics and the ways to become one. I adopted it here:

Here are the seven ways to be a good neighbor (what the Bible teaches us even through a pandemic.

Being a good neighbor can happen in a million different ways. Ask a few friends what it looks like to be a good neighbor and you're likely to get a dozen wonderful—yet different—answers. Endeavoring to be a good neighbor in any season, let alone during a global pandemic, presents as many opportunities as it does challenges.

It's important to ask: *Who is my neighbor? What are my responsibilities as a good neighbor? How do I connect with others and show them the hope I have in Christ?* As Christians, we are defined by our beliefs and how we live out our faith in front of others.

We look to God to teach and empower us to be good neighbors in word and deeds.

With our world in a state of uncertainty, we all need a reminder of who we're called to be. Together with Moody Radio, we went back to the Word of God to share some essential lessons on how to be good neighbors. Throughout the Bible, God continually gives attention to the posture (or heart) of man before speaking to the actions of man (Matt. 12:34b). With this framework in mind, we present seven ways the Bible teaches us to be good neighbors in posture and in practice.

Four Biblical Postures of a Good Neighbor

1. Love God first

"Love the Lord your God with all your heart and with all your soul and with all your mind." This is the first and greatest commandment. —Matthew 22:37–38 (NIV)

The starting place for being a good neighbor is loving God with all that we are. The applications of this love are endless, but He is the first focus and recipient of our love.

2. Love your neighbor as yourself

Jesus continues speaking to the Sadducees in Matthew 22:39 by saying, "And the second [commandment] is like it: 'Love your neighbor as yourself.'" After stating that the greatest commandment is to love God, Jesus tells His people that their next greatest responsibility is to love their neighbor as dearly as they love themselves.

3. Love your neighbor as Christ loved you

Jesus commands His people to love their neighbors as they love themselves. In John 13:34–35, just before the feast of the Passover, before He is betrayed by Judas and subsequently hung on a cross, Jesus elevates the love we are to have for our neighbors by giving a new command: "Love one another. As I have loved you, so you must love one another. By this, everyone will know that you are my disciples if you love one another."

Jesus's command to love as He loved us is further demonstrated in John 15:13 (NIV): "Greater love has no one than this: to lay down one's life for one's friends."

4. Be a Good Samaritan

This final biblical posture builds upon the first two by answering the question, "Who is my neighbor?" An expert in the law asks this question of Jesus in Luke 10:25–37. Jesus responds by telling him the parable of the Good Samaritan. In the parable, a despised Samaritan helps an injured Jewish man whom both a priest and a Levite have chosen to ignore.

The Samaritan bandages the injured man's wounds and takes him to an inn where he pays for his continued care. Jesus, in telling the parable, changes the lawyer's question from, "Who is my neighbor?" to, "Which of these three was a neighbor?" The lawyer rightly identifies the unlikely character, the Samaritan, as the one who displayed mercy. Jesus is telling the lawyer that he must love anyone he comes across with the same care, mercy, and generosity displayed by the Samaritan.

Three Biblical practices of a good neighbor

1. Pray for your neighbors by name (James 5:16b, Matt 6:5)

Whether for a coworker, a friend, or a literal next-door neighbor, you can practice being a good neighbor by praying for the people God has placed in your life. The better you know your neighbor, the more specifically you can pray for them. Pray for their family, career, and health. Ask God to bless them—physically and spiritually—and incorporate Scriptures like Ephesians 1:15–19 into your prayers.

2. Inquire and listen (Luke 3:10-11, Matt. 25:44-45, Phil. 2:4)

The better you know your neighbor, the more intentional you will be in praying for them. Ask, *how can I pray for you? In what ways do you need encouragement? Will you share with me what you've been going through?* Simple questions encourage others to share their stories and needs. Ask God for wisdom to know when to offer words of life and when to simply listen. Be prepared to emulate the Samaritan by offering the same compassion and willingness to sacrificially care for your neighbor's needs.

3. Respond (2 Cor. 9:6-8, 1 Thess. 5:11, Prov. 19:17, Gal. 6:2, Heb. 13:16)

The Samaritan didn't just offer the injured man his pity; he also tended to his physical needs. It may not be your place to provide for all your neighbor's needs, but simply offering an uplifting word or tangible gift can alleviate many hardships. Whether being a good neighbor means speaking words of encouragement or paying for a tank of gas, remember Jesus's words: "'Truly I tell you, whatever you did for one of the least of these brothers and sisters of mine, you did for me'" (Matt. 25:40; NIV).

CHAPTER EIGHT
Mister Rogers and Jesus Christ: The Nifty Neighbors

Looking at the well-lived lives of our two nifty neighbors, we see some important "common denominators" that I believe we can learn from and live with. Their lives were the best examples of lives lived accordingly, anchored on virtues, values, high moral standards. Their love for people, their interactions, and their actions moved, motivated, and inspired many lives.

The more I look at the lives of our two personalities, Jesus and Mister Rogers, I see more of a similarity than a difference. Mister Rogers embodied a Christ-like attitude being a Christian Minister himself, and this must be one reason why I see Christ in his life. Mister Rogers embodies the values of Christ in his episodes and it is evident.

Putting Mister Rogers' religious affiliation aside, and focusing on his messages, we can make various connections to the good aspects of their lives and come to a conclusion: that Jesus and Mister Rogers impacted the lives of people who knew them and successfully achieved their individual mission in life.

These great characteristics embody our two nifty neighbors:

1. On Breaking the Barriers of Race, Color, Background

Mr. François Clemmons, a black American, took the role of the resident cop in the series. At first, he said, he had apprehensions. "I grew up in the Ghetto so I did not have a positive opinion about police officers. I really had a hard time putting myself in that role, so I was not excited to become Officer Clemmons at all," Clemmons said in a TV interview.

Clemmons eventually accepted the role and became the first African-American man to have a recurring role in a children's television series. "There are black kids watching the show who needed a black figure who will not let them down," he said.

One of the most unforgettable appearances of Officer Clemmons was in Episode 195 aired in May 1969 when Mister Rogers invited him to share a kiddie pool with him on a hot summer day. As mentioned in Chapter 5, this episode was aired during the 1960s where there exists pool segregation between whites and blacks. In the scene, Officer Clemmons said this after Mister Rogers invited him to dip his feet in the pool, "It looks enjoyable, but I don't have a towel or anything." Mister Rogers said, "We can share mine!" The two enjoyed dipping their feet together in the same small pool – a symbolic and humble act from Mister Rogers that broke the barriers of race and color, which showed the world that we are all equal. Other than this, Mister Rogers also changed Mr. Clemmons' perspective in life.

Jesus and the Bible also share the same idea and support for racial equality. One of the early church's leaders, Paul, wrote about racial divisions which happened in Jesus' time.

In the first century AD, it was common to assign different values to different races and ethnicities. In an article by NewSpring Church, it says, "Foreigners, women, and children were generally regarded as property owned by the male heads of households and local rulers. Foreigners would often be employed in bonded labor (enslavement to pay off debts, like Jesus mentioned in Matthew 18:21-35), making it difficult or impossible to live freely.

At that time, one of the primary divisions in the church was between Jews and Gentiles. Some Jews who had joined the movement of Christianity were trying to force non-Jewish (Gentile) believers to perform Jewish rituals. They argued that to be a good Christian, they had to do all the right Jewish religious activities, too.

Rather than telling Christians to ignore the discrimination against Gentiles, Paul addressed it head-on: "There is no difference between Jew and Gentile—the same Lord is Lord of all and richly blesses all who call on him" (Romans 10:12).

We see this echoed later when Philip, also a leader of the church, helps an Ethiopian eunuch understand part of the Bible and begin following Jesus (Acts 8:26-40). Other people don't determine our value; God does."

2. On Self-Identity and Self-Worth

Mister Rogers and Jesus Christ made us feel our true worth. They boosted our faith in ourselves, and made us identify who we really are and what we are capable of – that we are capable of bigger things! We are valuable in the eyes of society and of God!

Jesus taught the value of each person in the eyes of God. Jesus taught that a long time ago, even before God created you and before He created this universe, you were the focus of His love. In Ephesians 1:4, "He chose us in Him before the foundation of the world, that we should be holy and without blame before Him in love"

Jesus also taught that as one loved by God, you have also been chosen by God for "adoption as sons by Jesus Christ to Himself" (Ephesians 1:5 NIV). This adoption came at a high price, the death of His Son. "He made us accepted in the Beloved. In Him we have redemption through His blood, the forgiveness of sins" (Ephesians 1:6, 7 NIV).

As a person who is loved by God and adopted into His family, you can be sure that God has a plan for your life: "In Him also we have obtained an inheritance, being predestined according to the purpose of Him who works all things according to the counsel of His will, that we who first trusted in Christ should be to the praise of His glory" (Ephesians 1:11, 12 NIV).

Mister Rogers also made his viewers feel valued – that they are capable of what they set their minds to. In one of Mister Rogers' episodes entitled, *"Feeling Good About Who We Are,"* he showed a hula hoop and tried to practice it until he was able to perform it. At the end of the segment, he had his parting words saying, "I'd like to think of children who are just learning to walk. They don't wear any magic hats, they just toddle and fall, and get up and toddle again."

He continued, "Somehow, inside of us, we know what we're able to do. And we just keep trying until we finally learn. When you do that with the things that you can learn, I'm really proud of you."

Mister Rogers repeats these lines, again and again: "You've made this day a special day by just your being you. There is no person in the whole world like you, and I like you just the way you are."

3. On Love, Kindness, and Goodness in General

Many of Mister Rogers' episodes talked about the values of kindness, humility, patience, perseverance, courage, respect, hardwork. In his 30 years in television, there are too many great lessons that we can mention. But I believe the very essence of these episodes and lessons is rooted more in goodness and kindness.

In an article in The Gospel Coalition website, it says: Ultimately Rogers had a humble and applaudable goal with his show: to create TV that made goodness look attractive. Going against the grain of children's programming that often glorified cynicism, childishness, and other bad behavior (for example, *The Simpsons*, *Rugrats*, much of Nickelodeon, and so on), Rogers was unapologetically committed to modeling virtue, respect, growth, maturity. He didn't think goodness needed to be presented with a wink. He found no fault in presenting a "neighborhood" vision that was idealistic, almost eschatological.

Jesus on the other hand, spread the good news to humanity through spreading love for every person, care for the oppressed, compassion for the poor and sick, and concern for the sinners. He showed mercy to the unheard voices, and became the voice of the people. Amidst the oppression of religious leaders, He stood firm and never faltered in His teachings of love. In His last breaths, He still "killed them with kindness." This kindness extended even while he was facing death for something He did not deserve.

Figure 8. A re-enactment of Jesus' crucifixion and death in the year AD 33.

While He was being crucified, He said "Father, forgive them, for they do not know what they are doing'" (Luke 23:34). The declaration of their need for forgiveness makes it clear that they were guilty, despite their ignorance. Some sins we willingly and rebelliously commit; others we are entirely unaware of. How kind it was for Jesus to ask forgiveness for those who oppressed him.

The same message was spread by our good neighbor, Mister Rogers. In his speech, Fred Rogers said, "A lot of people asked me if I've ever been mad, yes of course. Everybody gets mad sometimes. The important thing is what we do at the mad that we feel in life," with the encouragement to forgive those who wronged you.

In a song, Mister Rogers' shares his good heart and kindness by teaching us patience. He wrote a song *"What Do You Do With The Mad That You Feel"* which he sang on one of the episodes of his program:

What Do You Do With The Mad That You Feel?

Composed and performed by Fred Rogers
What do you do with the mad that you feel
When you feel so mad you could bite?
When the whole wide world seems oh, so wrong...
And nothing you do seems very right?
What do you do? Do you punch a bag?
Do you pound some clay or some dough?
Do you round up friends for a game of tag?

Or see how fast you go?
It's great to be able to stop
When you've planned a thing that's wrong,
And be able to do something else instead
And think this song:
I can stop when I want to
Can stop when I wish
I can stop, stop, stop any time.
And what a good feeling to feel like this
And know that the feeling is really mine.
Know that there's something deep inside
That helps us become what we can.
For a girl can be someday a woman
And a boy can be someday a man.

4. Broke the Barriers, Formed a Radical Movement

We studied in the previous chapters how Jesus formed his radical movement through his teachings. Born in an era where religious leaders apply strict rules and stiff moral uprightness, Jesus' teachings are considered out of the norm, borderline laughable, and antagonistic. He was a misfit. A square peg in a round whole.

Jesus' message was a form of protest against the church traditions without literally protesting them loudly and openly. Instead, He used His miracles and parables with His disciples to show His antagonism to the religious structure of the time. He introduced a new set of ways – forgiveness of sins and the acceptance of sinners to the kingdom of God.

Yes. Forgiveness was one of Jesus' major important teaching that brought religious leaders dismay. Jesus had several stories of forgiveness. One of those is written in Matthew 6:14 which says, "For if you forgive other people when they sin against you, your heavenly Father will also forgive you."

Repentance of sins and forgiving those who wronged as a pre-requisite to the Father's forgiveness were some of the basic principles that Jesus taught. This brought religious teachers to cry foul over. This can be seen in a story written in Mark 9:1-8: Jesus stepped into a boat, crossed over, and came to His own town. Some men brought to Him a paralytic, lying on a mat. When Jesus saw their faith, He said to the paralytic, "Take heart, son; your sins are forgiven."

At this, some of the teachers of the Law said to themselves, "This fellow is blaspheming!" Knowing their thoughts, Jesus said, "Why do you entertain evil thoughts in your hearts? Which is easier: to say, 'Your sins are forgiven,' or to say, 'Get up and walk'?

But so that you might know that the Son of Man has authority on earth to forgive sin..." Then He said to the paralytic, "Get up, take your mat, and go home." And the man got up and went home. When the crowd saw this, they were filled with awe, and they praised God, who had given such authority to men.

Jesus' radical mindset and perspective became a source of angst among leaders. But despite this, Jesus trod on His mission even if it cost Him His own life.

Both Rogers and Jesus made an indelible mark in history by shifting the course of destiny. Without Christ's radical mindset and actions, we would still be living in the old ways of tradition that punish the sinner, not the sin.

Without Rogers' radical teachings, millions of children would have lived differently with intolerance, and a lack of childhood foundations of values of love and kindness.

What are you willing to let go to help others?

CHAPTER NINE
So What?

"For a girl can be someday a woman And a boy can be someday a man."
-Mister Rogers

As I write this book, I've also been amazed at how our nifty neighbors broke the walls of division and opened the gates of love. Even as I end this book with this last chapter, I still could not fathom enough the kind of person our nifty neighbors are. Their goodness is too deep, and their love is too wide. Their lives cannot be explained thoroughly because their impact on the world created millions of stories that outpower our ability to comprehend.

I believe that not all readers share the same religious belief or faith as Mister Rogers, Jesus Christ, or myself. We have varying beliefs and personalities. But let us remember and put in mind that *love and kindness* are elements that require no criteria – no age, sex, religion, or status. We can all share *love and kindness*, spread it, and make it known to the world regardless of our varying faiths. This is what can bind us together.

As I wrote at the beginning of this book, this world is divided. Media, politics, religion – let's face it. These aspects of our society contributed to a better society but it built a wall between us that has hardened through the years. Every day, we become different than alike. Technology broke us apart rather than united us all. We aim for validation; we aim to be recognized. These are not the kind of values our nifty neighbors would like us to live by.

So, I challenge you to take that first step. Rather than focusing on our differences, lets continue to find common ground. We needed the stories of Mister Rogers and Jesus to show us how their stories became an instrument of unity and peace. We can only be united when we stick to our common core – love. The lives of our nifty neighbors perfectly magnify to us the kind of life we should live – connected in love, kindness, respect, tolerance, acceptance, and encouragement. Supporting each other. Lifting each other up.

Motivating one another. Inspiring each other. Providing for each other.

Let's start by doing something good today to a friend or neighbor. Make them smile. Make they day. Help a stranger. Complement them. Make them feel valued and loved.

I hope that their stories will continually teach us that we can change ourselves for the better. Together, we can create a society that is radical for the good. Even as grown-ups, there are many different lessons that we can still learn from Mister Rogers. and Jesus. We can still personify these lessons in our lives today. Yes, let's start today!

Remember what Jesus said in His teachings:

At that time the disciples came to Jesus, saying, "Who is the greatest in the kingdom of heaven?" And calling to him a child, he put him in the midst of them and said, "Truly, I say to you, unless you turn and become like children, you will never enter the kingdom of heaven." (Matthew 18:1-3).

When we train our minds to be receptive to the lessons that are exposed in this book – like the mind of a child that's always willing to explore, to be open, and to be receptive – we can achieve the greatest reward from God himself. If you think it doesn't come from God, well, humanity will soon reward your humanity.

Every day, we face various challenges and hardships that test our faith, patience, and our humanity. But here's one more challenge. Ask yourself. Now that I know the two nifty neighbors:

What would Mister Rogers do? What would Jesus do?

www.ingramcontent.com/pod-product-compliance
Lightning Source LLC
Chambersburg PA
CBHW020336130626
46549CB00003B/1192